King's Lynn in the 1930s

by

Bob Booth

<u>Dedication</u>

To the memory of Robert (Bob) Nixon

Tricky Sam Publishing

1801 . . . 10,000

annum for 40 years on condition that the Council contributed £3 15s. per year and let the h...

bought these houses as a speculation. Scores of them have changed h...

Landlords

August 8, 1933. THE LYNN NEWS AND COUNTY PRESS

HOW LYNN'S COURTS AND ALLEYS WILL BE SWEPT AWAY

ALL ABOUT COUNCIL'S £200,000 SCHEME

What Lynn Will Look Like In Five Years

NEW HOUSES FOR NINE PER CENT. OF POPULATION

Slum Clearance Committee's Comprehensive Plans

OUR GREAT PROBLEM in dealing with slum clearance is that of old people; sometimes one person living alone and sometimes two persons—often old age pension-

THE LYNN NEWS AND COUNTY PRESS

HOUSES LYNN COUNCIL WOULD LIKE TO DEMOLISH

Some of the Courts and Yards to be Discussed at To-day's Ministry Inquiry

them to the magistrates or County Court."

"The Town Clerk: They will have to appeal to the Ministry at a local inquiry.

Mr. Carpenter's Amendment

way clear to running a service along there. I hope that the council will help us to help the Government to fill this long standing need."

ALD. SKINNER CONSULTS NUTTALL!

larger ... ... upy-ing the houses to the new areas, and under certain circumstances the committee would be prepared to grant an extended life to these properties.

Personally I would advise such owners to communicate with the Town Clerk and give such an undertaking. The committee can say at once whether they consider the houses suitable for the pur-

HOW LYNN'S SLUMS WILL BE CLEARED

RE-HOUSING 1,900 TENANTS

The Corporation's Scheme Clearly Explained

BY J. HARWOOD CATLEUGH

(Chairman of the Lynn Slum Clearance Committee)

[in an address to the Lynn Round Table members.]

THE BEST WAY to appreciate Lynn's slum clearance problem is to go back and see the origin of the slums themselves. In the 18th Century Lynn was a walled town, intersected by three waterways, the Millfleet, the Purfleet, and the Fisher fleet.

THE LYNN NEWS AND COUNTY PRESS

SOME HOUSES WHICH WILL BE DEMOLISHED

How The Town Has Grown

Slum Dwellers Fare Worse Than Gorillas!

Vicar's Thoughtful Sermon To Mayor and Corporation

THE MAYOR OF LYNN (Mr. T. A. Frost), the Mayoress and members of the Corporation attended morning service at St. Margaret's...

need for better housing conditions and the abolition of slums.

In dealing with these four points the Vicar paid tribute to the reso-

Photo: Goodchild, Lynn.

Typical examples of the 512 houses which will be demolished under the Council's slum clearance scheme. There are 320 back-to-back houses in the borough. The only light in those houses comes from the front window and doorway. There is no back door and no window in the back room.

Introduction

King's Lynn in the 1930s

The photographs in this book record a number of the yards, courts, squares and lanes as they were in the mid 1930s. Many of those pictured here were due to be demolished before the end of the decade.

In August 1933 the Lynn Town Council had passed the Slum Clearance Scheme which would provide new homes (512 houses) for those that were considered to be living in "undesirable conditions" and "unfit for human habitation". This involved moving 1890 men, women and children (9% of the town's population) to new houses to the South and North of the town.

The land used for the building of the houses was to be between Wisbech Road & Saddlebow Road (approximately 200 homes) and land between Salter's Road & Estuary Road (approximately 300 homes).

Under an earlier Act (1924) the council had already built 318 new homes since 1927 and had re-housed 1200 of the town's population.

Most of the areas for demolition involved small numbers of houses and the only large area was around Bridge Street where 49 of the 89 houses were to be pulled down. It was planned to re-house families at the rate of approximately 100 per year over 5 years. The five year plan was scheduled to be completed by March 1938.

I have tried to list the occupants of the various yards etc. at the time the pictures were taken.

Obviously over a two or three year span there was movement by the occupants so this is not a precise snapshot of yard and householder. Only the principal householder is listed and, therefore, there is no indication of how many residents there were in each house. In fact there was no serious over-crowding, the average was less than 3½ persons per house.

Sometimes there is no householder listed, usually because the house was empty, or the house was let in weekly tenements, or the information was refused.

Acknowledgements

Almost all the photographs were originally taken by PM Goodchild & Sons.

Thanks to the following for all their help and encouragement:
Dick Goodchild.
Susan Maddock (Principal Archivist, Norfolk Record Office), Norwich.
The Lynn News.
Eva and Roger Carter (for their help in naming some of the yards).
Ken and Jill Smith.
Vera and Derek Witt.
Brian Stock (King's Lynn Borough Council).
All the staff at Central Library, King's Lynn.
King's Lynn Borough Archives at the Old Gaol House, King's Lynn.
Colin Bailey (Dawbarns Pearson, King Street).

Maps used by kind permission of Ordnance Survey, Southampton.

Copyright © Bob Booth 2006
First Printed 2006
Reprinted 2009
Published by Tricky Sam Publishing
Printed by Clanpress, King's Lynn
Tel: 01553 772737 Email: john@clanpress.co.uk

REPORT on:— 3, Burton's Court, New Conduit Street.

Re:— Slum Clearance.

Inspector:— H.G.Cobbold. Date:— 11th February, 1937.

Name and Address of Owner:— Mrs. Smith, Hunstanton. Type:— 2 storey, brick & tile.

Tenant:— Mr. Murray. Rent paid weekly:— 5/-

Sub-Tenant (if any) Rent paid weekly:—

ROOM	Height ft. ins.	Floor Area sq. ft.	Occupants		If Over-crowded	Occupier	Type of Window	Window Area sq. ft.	Window Opening sq. ft
			Adults	Children					
Living room	8.2	190					S) -)	16.8 2.7	O.H. fixed
Bedroom	8.3	185	2		No.	Mr. Murray.	S	16.19	O.H.
Attic	5.10	72					C	6.6	O.H.

	ADULTS M F	CHILDREN M F	TOTAL
Number of occupants:—	1 1		2

Sanitary accommodation:—W.C.:— 2 water closets for four houses.

Refuse Receptacle:— 2 dustbins for four houses. D.P.C.:— no evidence.

Yard Paved or unpaved:— defective. Any Sink:— none.

Copper:— Wash-house in yard-sole use, copper, brick floor and door defective. Water Supply:— 2 taps in yard to four houses.

Storage of Food:— unventilated store.

Ventilation:— No through ventilation. Cooking:— Cooking range in L.R.

Defects :—

G. Floor:— L.R:- Defective sash cords; wall and ceiling plaster; floorboards; Cupboard door under stairs; walls damp.

Stairs:- 1st & 2nd flights:- wall and ceiling plaster defective; damp walls.

1st Floor:—B.R:- Defective ceiling plaster; damp and defective wall plaster; defective floorboards; defective window frame and sashcords; insufficient window space and opening.

2nd Floor:—Attic:- Defective wall and ceiling plaster; defective floorboards; insufficient window space and opening.

External Walls bulging; brickwork perished; main roof defective; defective main and copper chimney stacks; absence of eaves gutters to water closet and wash-house, also rain water pipes. Yard and passage paving defective. Light obstructed with distances at front.

A report was generated for each property in order to show the exact state of that property. The above is a typical report and shows just what conditions were like. In this report there are only two outside lavatories and two outside taps to service four families.

ABOVE: Atto's Yard, Norfolk Street—this was next to 82, Norfolk Street—roughly where Lidl is now. Those listed living here were: Louisa Johnson, Roseanna Cooper, Annie Simpson, Robert Hammond, Edith Stolham, Victor Tudor, Herbert Norton, Jane Kent, James Gamble & Thomas Bishop. BELOW: Valentine's Yard, Norfolk Street.

California Yard (1), Norfolk Street. There were eleven householders here: Gertrude Blyth, Edna Baker, Lewis Hare, Susan Haverson, George Thurston, Frederick Haverson, Emma Eastwood, Benjamin Catchpole, Albert Green and Edith Hare. The yard was located between 104 & 105, Norfolk Street.

California Yard (2). There was no-one living at No.1 at this time - children are standing outside No.2. The householder was listed as Gertrude Blyth. Next door at No.3 lived Edna May Baker.

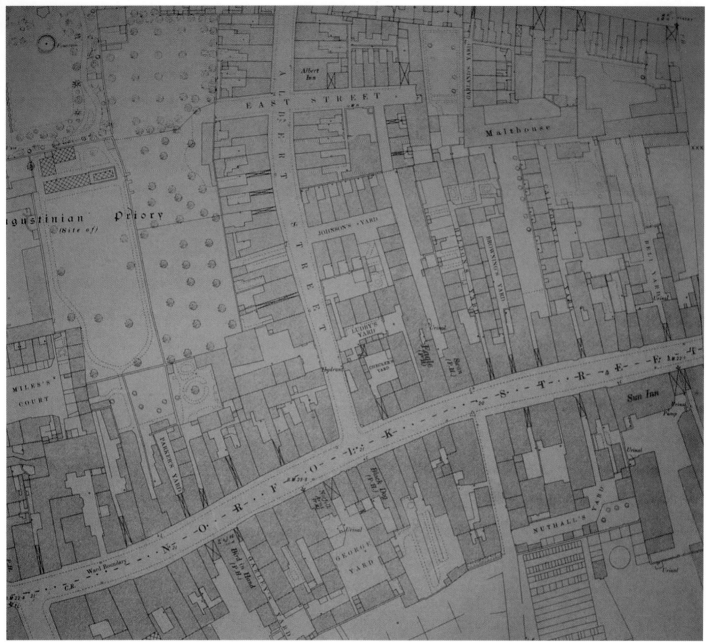

ABOVE:
A section from the Ordnance Survey map of the town, naming many of the yards.

Browning's Yard, Hildon's Yard, California Yard, Johnson's Square (or Johnson's Yard), Gazley's Yard, and Garland Yard are shown along with others.

RIGHT:
Gazley's Yard, beside 18, Norfolk Street, the only residents here were Emma Barley and Alice Futter.

This yard was next to the Bird-in-Hand public house whose landlord at the time was Eustace Horace Atkinson.

Browning's Yard, between 108 & 109, Norfolk Street There were seven families living here in the mid 1930's when this picture was taken. Listed were Elizabeth Rudd, Earnest Woodward, John Rudd, Sidney Price, Thomas Hardy, John Fox & Robert Ward.

Hildon's Yard, between 108 & 109, Norfolk Street Norfolk Street, next to Browning's Yard. This yard accounted for fourteen families. The principal householders were Walter Reed, Frederick Cheetham, Isaac Howe, Sarah Bailey, Albert Newdick, Robert Kent, Bertie Newdick, John McCowen, Horace Hewson, Joseph Brown, Frederick Hunt, Cecil Greeves, Fred Bracher and Samuel Mann.

ABOVE: Anchor of Hope Yard, between 95 & 96, Norfolk Street. Residents here were Walter Tann, William Kendle, Robert Rose, Arthur Wybrow, John Daw, William Allen & James Kinsella. BELOW: Lift's Yard. Also between 95 & 96, Norfolk Street. Only two residents listed about this time: George Baker & Thomas Hampson. There was also a slaughter-house in this yard!

RIGHT:
Garland Yard, Austin Street.
There were only four properties
here.
These were occupied by
William Hipkin, Robert Pratt,
George Hansell and Lily Fox.

BELOW:
East Place, East Street,
Albert Street.
This comprised three households:
George West lived at No.1,
Hermann Boormann at No.2
and James Cook at No.3.

ABOVE & BELOW: George Yard, (between 24 & 25, Norfolk Street). Sid Baker (above, holding trowel) attends to roof repairs. The principal householders living here at around this time: William Jubey, Robert Shallow, William Gill, Hannah Skipper, Frederick Sellers, Alexander Goldsmith, William Roper & Fanny Smith. WM Couperthwaite (ironmonger) had a workshop here. Ernest Winter's shop at 117, Norfolk Street can be seen through the archway (below).

ABOVE: 5 & 6, George Yard (between 24 & 25 Norfolk Street). Frederick Sellars and Alexander Goldsmith lived here.
BELOW: Johnson's Square or Johnson's Yard, Albert Street. There were 12 households here. Pictured are Nos. 10, 11 & 12.
Charlotte Bullen, Herbert Doy & Robert Gore lived here.

Rutter's Yard. This was between 43 and 44, Norfolk Street. It was home to three families -
householders listed were John Rose, Johanna Elizabeth Wiles and Edwin Victor Wiles.

Railway Passage, ran from 92, Norfolk Street to 88, Austin Street. All trace of this disappeared when John Kennedy Road was built. It was so named as it allowed access from Norfolk Street to the M&GN rail terminus (closed in 1886) in Austin Street.
There were thirteen properties here at this time—the residents were Mrs S Curson, Mrs Morley, Alfred Finney, Edward Page, Miss Rudd, GB Trew, Benjamin Winterton, Mrs Brookes, William Sands, William Cannell, Mrs Barnaby, Alfred Back and Fred Curtis.
BELOW LEFT: Looking towards Austin Street. BELOW RIGHT: Looking towards Norfolk Street.

ABOVE: Whitening Yard, between 24 & 26, North Street.

RIGHT:
Whitening Yard.
Living here were
Jack Brittain,
George Howlett
(Mrs Howlett is
leaning against
her front window),
Benjamin Bunns,
Cyril Briggs &
Arthur Shears.

BELOW:
Begley's Yard,
North Street.
Home to eight
families. Listed
householders were
Ernest Bone,
Charles Castleton,
George Eglinton,
Edward Gordon,
Archibald
Castleton,
Walter Hornigold,
Thomas Petts and
Frank Petts.

TOP: Another view of Begley's Yard, North Street.
BELOW: Watson's Yard, North Street. This was home to Thomas Ward, James Norris, James Greenwood and William Twite. St. Nicholas school can be seen in the background.

LEFT & RIGHT:

Devonshire's Yard.
This was between 20 & 22, North Street.

Access to many yards was down a narrow passage between buildings fronting a street - just enough room to push a pram or bike through (left)!

Listed householders were: Walter Ashby, Arthur Pemment, George Benefer, Arthur Colby, Arthur Wheeler & Ada Collis.

ABOVE: North Place, North Street. Living here at this time were Charles Fisher, Robert Fisher and Ralph Auker.
The following were living in flats here: John Cook, William Holden, Susanna Bailey, Elijah Holden Jnr., Edith Hillard, James Bone, Alfred Mann & Elijah Holden Snr.
BELOW: Churchman's Yard, North Street. Residents — Phoebe Colby, Harry Kirby & David Jary.

ABOVE: Hanover Yard, next to 7, St. Ann's Street. The only occupant (in the house on the right) living in this yard at this time was Arthur Petts. The house on the left had been the home of Mrs Dexter.

RIGHT: Hanwell's Yard, Pilot Street. This was the home of Stanley Griffin, John Day and Henry Stevens and was situated between 38 & 40, Pilot Street. The yard was next door but one to the Fisherman's Arms, whose landlord was Abel Garnett.

LEFT: Chapel Yard, next to 1, Pilot Street. This was the home of Henry Fryer, William Rudd, Robert Bailey and Phoebe Massingham. At the end of the yard is St. Nicholas School. RIGHT: Bird's Yard, between 18 & 20, Pilot Street. Inhabitants here were Rose Jarvis, John Smith, John Reed, Percy Allen and Wilfred Watts..

23

Rhodes Yard. This was between 32 & 34, Pilot Street. It was home to Thomas Brightmore Jnr., Albert Henry Goldsmith, Francis Back and James Collison.

ABOVE: Hart's Yard, Pilot Street. On a busy Monday morning. Householders listed were William Foster, Cyril Fuller, Wilfred Burch & Frank Fisher.
LEFT & BELOW: Grampus Yard, Pilot Street.

TOP: 46 & 48, Pilot Street. These were both unoccupied at the time.
ABOVE: 24, Pilot Street. Listed as 'bungalow - yard'. Mr A Gray lived here.

UPPER RIGHT & BELOW:
Half Moon Yard, Pilot Street.
Three householders listed here:
Herbert Hudson, George Hardy &
Phoebe Dix.

RIGHT:
1a-2a, North End
Yard. Mr Anderson
lived at 1a and Mrs
Kirby lived at 2a.
Living down North
End Yard were
Charles Smith,
Sarah Kirby,
Albert Bassett,
Leah Senter,
Walter Goodson,
James Jary,
Thomas Smith,
James Castleton,
Rosetta Miller,
Rose Collison,
Elizabeth Bailey,
Frank Castleton,
Frederick Allen,
Frederick Earl,
William Day,
Herbert Akers and
Arthur Stevens.

LEFT: Sackers Buildings, St Nicholas Street. Householders here were Elizabeth Moy, Edward Guy, John Guy and Albert Shread. RIGHT: Burrell's Yard, St Ann's Fort, St.Ann's Street.

ABOVE: Seed's Yard, St. Nicholas Street. This was situated behind the Duke of Connaught pub (landlord Alfred Fuller).
The only residents living here at this time were John & Lavinia Setchell at No.2. Ravenshaw's Yard can be seen in the background.

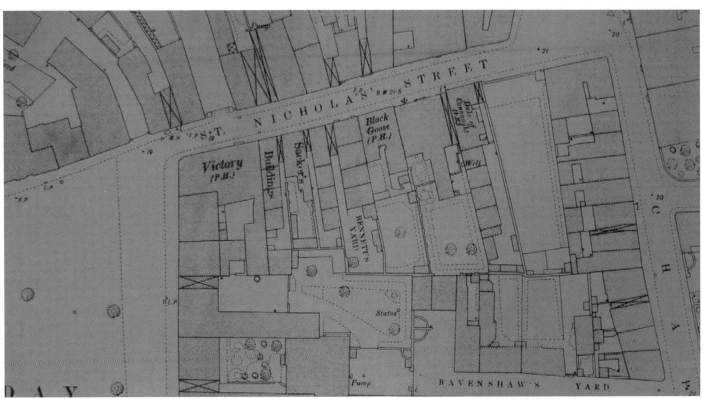

RIGHT: Bennett's Yard, St.Nicholas Street. This was situated between 20 & 22, St.Nicholas Street. The homes of James Greenwood and Robert Pottle were here.

BELOW: Chapel Yard, St. Ann's Street. Householders were James Holden, Rebecca Gent, Albert Hansell, Margaret Cook, Edith Fenn, Mary Bailey & Robert Tunstead.

St. Nicholas school can be seen in the background.

ABOVE:
Edward's Yard.
This was off
Market Lane which
runs between the
Tuesday Market
Place & Chapel
Street.

The yard has been
swallowed up by
the Dukes Head car
park.

Occupants at this
time were James
Whitfield, William
Norris and Harry
Clover.

ABOVE & BELOW: Miles Court (or Miles Square). This was between 13 & 16, Chapel Street. Householders were Alfred Stacey, Sidney Burch, Alfred Leggett, Charles Roper, James Steele, John Hardy, John Dexter, William Briggs, Edward Culpitt, Emma Anderson, Elizabeth Mawby, George Seaman & Sarah Howard.

ABOVE: Ravenshaw's Yard,
Chapel Street. This, like Chapel
Buildings, was located opposite the
current King's Lynn Borough Council
offices.
It lists as it's occupants: John Sainty,
William Wilfred, Cyril Franklin,
Richard Alexander (workshop),
Alfred Wenn (Top End),
Joseph Gawthorpe (Holyoake House)
& Frank Fysh (Ravenshaw's House).

RIGHT: Chapel Buildings,
Chapel Street.
Only two householders here:
Edward Daisley & Albert Seaman.

Cross Yard - between 4 & 7, Littleport Street . The busy shop opposite (which is still there today) was owned at this time by Lily Braybrooke. Living here were Sarah Bevis, Mary Williamson, Abraham Gray, William Lake and James Sainty.

Skipper's Yard - next to 2, Littleport Street. This was almost opposite Cross Yard. It was home to Elizabeth Ellender, John Dye, William Kendle & George Mansell.

ABOVE: Town centre. This area is bounded by Tower Street, New Conduit Street and High Street.
The Ordnance Survey map pre-dates this era. Baly's & Adcock's Yards were replaced by the Majestic in an earlier slum clearance.
BELOW: Cross Lane, Sedgeford Lane. The Majestic cinema is in the background (right).

RIGHT & BELOW:
Cross Lane, Sedgeford Lane. Both ends of Sedgeford Lane are still visible today. It ran from between 25 & 26, High Street to meet Tower Street beside the Majestic Cinema (built in 1928).

As can be seen , the lane ran behind the cinema.

Occupants were Isabel Greeves, William Allard, Richard Holmes, James Cave, James Reed, William Collier, Thomas English and Leslie Marsters.

Mill's Yard, between 12 & 13, Sedgeford Lane. The yard was divided into: *Centre Part* (residents - Charles Chapman, Rose Gilbert, Venus Empson & George Chilvers), *Top End* (residents - Elizabeth Valvona, Frederick Rust & Robert Collison) and *Side Yard* (residents - John Terelinck, Sidney Fox, Florence Fickling & Harold Blyth). The Majestic can be seen in the background.

ABOVE & BELOW: Mill's Yard, Sedgeford Lane.

Across the other side of Tower Street from Sedgeford Lane was South Clough Lane, another community in itself. This picture shows Mount Pleasant in Regent Street. Residents of Mount Pleasant included Stanley Hitchcock, Robert Yallop, John Bird and Bernard Hirst. This whole area is now occupied by the town baths and new multi-storey car-park.

ABOVE: This map shows more of the South Clough Lane community.
BELOW: Whincop Place, Whincop Street, South Clough Lane. This bungalow is probably 'Hope Cottage' owned by Lewis Pipe. The centre of the map is where the new multi-storey car-park is now located.

LEFT: Trundle's Yard, between 45 & 47, South Clough Lane. This was the home of Albert Farrow. RIGHT: Whincop Place. Living here were Francis Wright, John Simpson, Herbert Youngs, Albert Sheppardson, William Bocking, James Sayer, John Frost, Thomas Rains, Horace Pearman, Annie Fisher, Fanny Barnes, John Stebbings, Frederick Bell, Joseph Anderson, Samuel Daisley & Bertie Collison.

ABOVE:
10 to 13, Stanley
Square,
Stanley Street
(from 57, Railway
Road).
Residents were
Alfred Pottle,
James Westmorland,
Margret Palmer and
Robert White.
In the background can
be seen the works of
Mark and John
Whitmore in nearby
Wellesley Street.

LEFT: Wilson's Flats,
between 27 & 28,
Broad Street.
Occupants were
Robert Whiley,
Kenneth Rout,
George Eglen,
Edith Maddison
and
Alfred Calton.

ABOVE: Bath's Yard, between 20 &21, Broad Street. Opposite was the Electric Cinema, later to become Taylor's Garage. The yard was approximately where the flyover now crosses the street. TA Furbank (funeral directors & builders) was at the end of the yard. Walter Lock had a garage here. Residents were George Curson, Alfred Hooks, Edward Tann, Albert Hornigold and Charles Barnes.

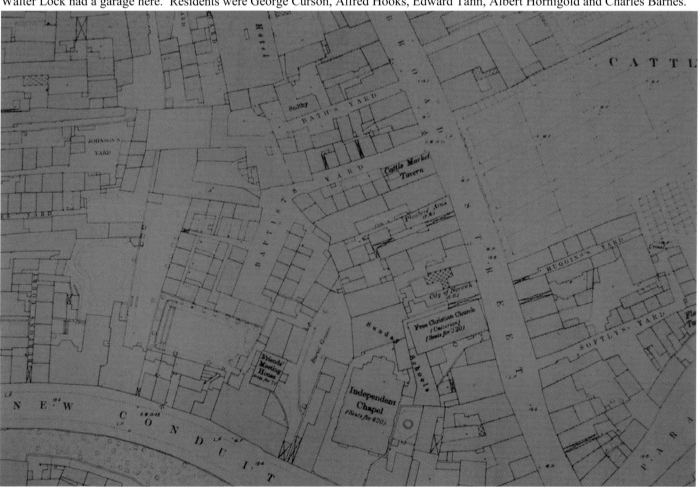

RIGHT:
Baptist's Yard
(or Baptist Chapel
Yard),
This was between
23 & 24, Broad
Street.
24, Broad Street
was the 'Cattle
Market' Tavern.
The landlord at
the time was
Edward Goodson.

Residents here
were:
Arthur Sainty,
Ernest Britton,
Reginald Howard,
George Smith,
Jane Rye,
Alfred Manning,
George Capps,
Arthur Pottle,
George Holland,
William Curry,
Herbert Cook,
Agnes Fisher,
Thomas Baxter,
Mary Russell,
William Cook,
Daisy Bligh &
George Youngs.

Hector Crome also
had workshops
here.

45

LEFT: Baptist's Yard, Broad Street.

BELOW: A letter of protest to the Lynn News about the impending Slum Clearance.

A TENANT'S PROTEST

SIR,—May I, as one who for 39 years has lived in Baptist Chapel-yard, Lynn, protest against the plans of the Lynn Corporation in regard to slum-clearance? My husband and I have brought up a healthy family of eight and we feel it would be a sin and a shame for our old cottage to be pulled down. There are two rooms upstairs, windows at the back and front, a convenience and a fair-sized yard.

For a long time now my husband has been out of work. We exist on a pension of 10s a week (5s. of which goes in rent) and if I live for another six years I shall qualify for a pension too. Does the Corporation think if they move us against our wishes that we could do more? Would they advise us to go "on the rates"—an indignity that would be unbearable?

With one or two exceptions, the houses in our district are better built than many of the council houses. Two doctors have told me that Baptist Chapel-yard is one of the healthiest in the town.

What the corporation should do is to wait until men are working and earning enough to enjoy a decent livelihood for themselves and their families.

The next thing we shall be hearing of is a new Baptist Arcade or a Broadway Avenue.

Yours, etc.,
"FAIR PLAY."

BOTTOM: Surrey Square, Baptist's Yard. This was the home of Thomas Anderson, Robert Starling, John Ely, Emma Barley and Alfred Ely.

Softly's Yard (or Softley's Yard), between 7 & 8, Broad Street. The only residents here at this time were Walter Pottle, William Benjamin and Frederick King.

RIGHT: Bennett's Yard. This was between 18 & 20, Tower Street. Only Richard Benstead and Jas Norris lived here.

LEFT: Burton's Court, 5, New Conduit Street. The opening to Burton's Court is still visible today and is used for access to the rear of New Conduit Street & High Street. The residents included William Murray, Leslie Fox, Mary Woodhouse and Stanley Simpson. (see page 4).

BELOW: Arme's Yard, 9, High Street. This was next door to Jermyn's (Debenham's). These properties were at the end of the yard.

LEFT & RIGHT:

Two more pictures of Arme's Yard, High Street. The picture on the left (looking towards High Street) is the front of the houses whilst the rear of the houses is shown on the right.

This yard was home to Ernest Eke, Mrs M Smith, Tom Chilvers, Edward Woodhouse, Mrs Franklyn, Alfred Hall, Herbert Knowles, Mrs Bowman & Cecil Thorn.

Law's Yard, between 7 & 8, High Street. Residents were Walton Hardy, Edward Hughes, Horace Jary, Edward Mindham, Benjamin Tuck, Ellen Loasby, Horace Pearman, Florence Mayes, Charlotte Chapman, Richard Castle & Rebecca Flegg.

Law's Yard, High Street. This yard was originally called Norton's Yard (see map on page 49).

RIGHT: Dennis Yard,
passage at 40, King Street.
 Residents were
Arthur Fakenbridge,
Francis Holmes
and John Dennis.

BELOW: Kendrick's Yard,
between 20 & 21, High Street.

Home of Selina Barron
and Lydia Howard.

ABOVE: Lincoln's Yard, between 8 & 9, Purfleet Street. This ran down beside the Purfleet Tavern. This would have been approximately at the back of where Boots is today.
Residents were Michael Collins, George Rix & Caroline Stilwell.

LEFT: Purfleet Street looking towards High Street. Lincoln's Yard was off to the left - roughly where the bicycle is parked against the kerb. Just beyond was Exley's Yard.

Photo courtesy of Lynn News.

ABOVE: Little Chequer, Purfleet Place. Home to William Broughton & Thomas Doy.
RIGHT: May Cottages. Between 12 & 16, Nelson Street. Home to Isaac Taylor, Alfred Fenton & James Clements. These cottages still exist today.

BELOW: Bone's Yard, 32, Queen Street. Resident here were David Harwood, William Barrett, George Lovick & George Anderson.

Brown's Yard, between 18 & 20, St. James Street. Residents were John Calcott, Reginald Eagle and Kathleen Tann.

LEFT:
Tower Court, at 39, St James Street. Residents were Mrs Grummett, Mrs Hudson, Mrs A Flood, Theobald Hill and Victor Widdicombe.

In the background can be seen the Building Material Co. (KL) Limited.

RIGHT:
Payne's Court, at 10, Church Street. Almost opposite Priory Lane. This was home to Ernest Russell, George Grummett, Dick Rye, Arthur Allen, Fred Rumble, George Reeve, Charles Buck, Philip High & Charles Simpson.

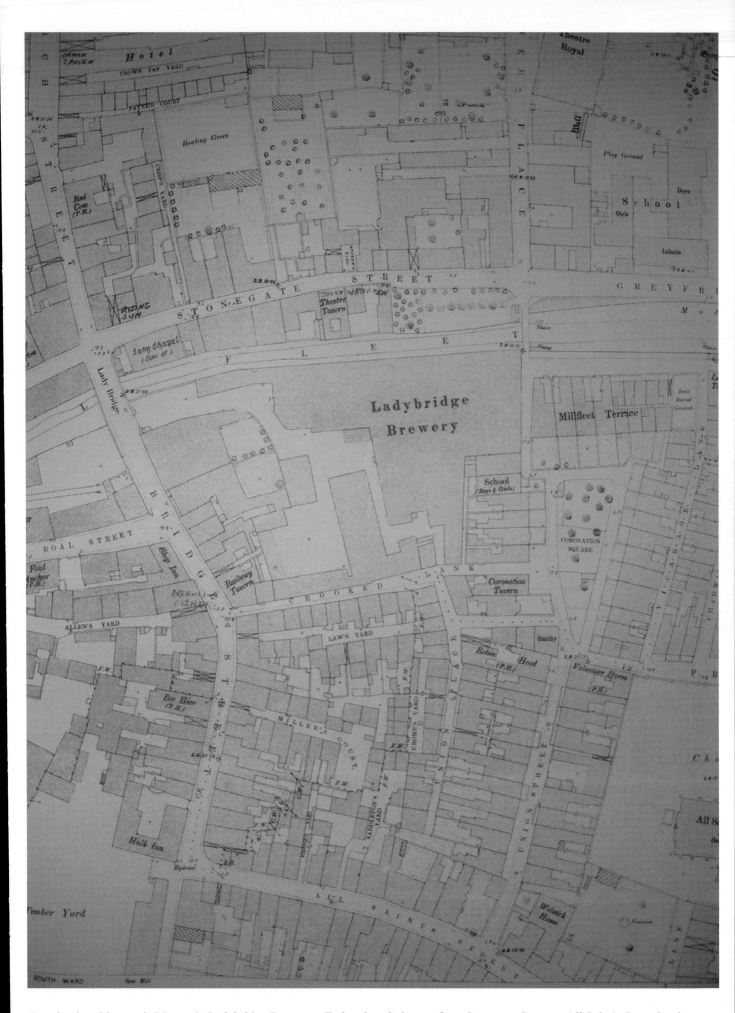

Dominating this map is Morgan's Ladybridge Brewery. Today the whole area from Stonegate Street to All Saint's Street has been replaced with Hillington Square. Payne's Court (previous page) can be seen top left. The following ten pages are all represented on this map.

3 & 4, Stonegate Street. Mr Cox and Mr George Harrison lived here.

1a & 2a, Bridge Street. The homes of Charles Scott and Edward Garner. All Saint's Street is to the right of the picture.

2 to 5, All Saint's Street. The homes of Robert Johnson, Harlock Human, Ernest Purdy and Thomas Sneesby.
The trade bike is leaning against AW Arrowsmith's (butchers) shop which is next to No.2. On the extreme right of the picture is the Anchor Pub.

ABOVE: Crisp's Yard, between 8 & 9, Stonegate Street. Householders listed were Albert Dixon, Leonard Fisk & Reginald Cook.

LEFT: Simpson's Yard, between 14 & 15, All Saint's Street. This was home to Ernest Brown, Edward Ryan, Margaret Hudson and William Reddington.

Crooked Lane - this ran from Bridge Street to Coronation Square. Both the Greenland Fishery Museum and the chimney on the Boal Quay can be seen from here. Living here at this time were John Eastwood, Frederick Russell, Harry Brightwell, Mrs M Crow, Walter Whiley, Alfred Needham, John Green & Edward Woohouse. Fred Barnaby also had a warehouse here.

ABOVE & NEXT PAGE: Union Place, Crooked Lane. Named householders here were Oswald Bloye, William Edge, Robert Mitchell, James Snasdell & Edith Casey. Children pose for the cameraman.

LEFT:
Crome's Yard, from 7, Union Place. Residents here were Frank Main, Mrs Griffiths, Bert Ellis and Reginald Eglen.

BELOW:
Law's Yard, from 12, Bridge Street. Also known as Davy Law's Yard. Residents included John Thorn, Ernest Purdy, William Branham, Florence Moule, Robert Groom, James Nucoll, William Chapman and Herbert Panton.

ABOVE: Miller's Court, from 9a, Bridge Street. Living here were William Russell, Charles Gilmour and Fanny Cowen. BELOW & RIGHT: Pump Yard, Vicarage Lane. Home to Albert English, Mrs Curson, Mrs Withers and Alec Stephenson.

14 & 15, Vicarage Lane. From 13, Providence Street to the Millfleet. Homes of George Millington & Claude Howard.

RIGHT:
The map shows London Road with Providence Street off to the left.

BELOW:
Daisley's Buildings, Providence Street. This was just inside the street on the south side. Living here were Robert Wright, Priscilla Harper, Robert Farrow, Frederick Say, William Benefer, William Long, Emma Cooper, Allan Dybal, Ann Lyon, Lewis Oakes, George White, Thomas Hayes, John Gamble, Walter Hearle, Stanley Turnbull, Charles Hornsby & Frederick Funnell.

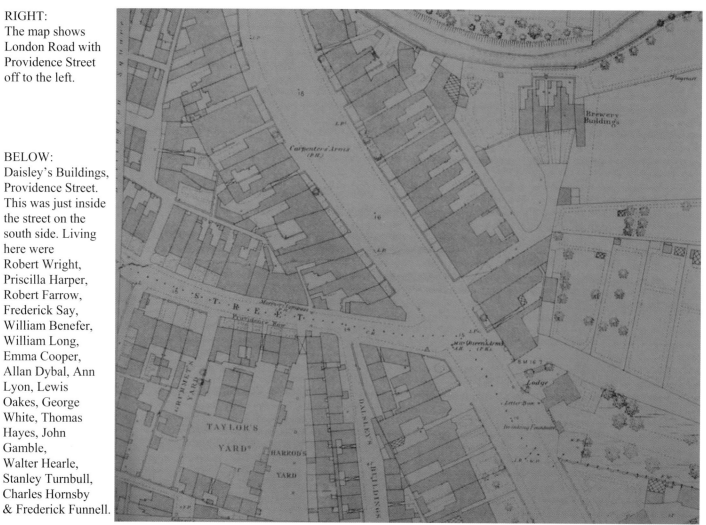

TOP & ABOVE: East Anglia Place, Providence Street.

BELOW: Dye's Buildings, North Everard Street.

North Everard Place, North Everard Street, No.6 was the home of Bertie Wakefield. Others who lived here were Charles Long (No.4), Henry Wales (No.5) & Herbert Wales (No.7). Also see next page.

ABOVE:
North
Everard
Place.

Henry
Long
(No.1)
&
Thomas
Pinner
(No.2)
lived here.

RIGHT:
No.3,
North
Everard
Place.
Charles
Simper
lived here.

RIGHT:
St. John's Cottages, from
5, John Street (originally
St. John's Street).
Living here were
Walter Barnes,
Frederick Smith and
Eleanor Brighton.

These cottages were also
known as St. John's
Yard.

RIGHT:
Frost's Yard. This was between 47 and 48,
South Everard Street.
Residents living here were Thomas Sharpin
and Mary Ann Elizabeth Ryan.

Outside lavatory in the right foreground.
The door is cut in order to give good
ventilation!

ABOVE & BELOW: Gilbert's Row, between 44 & 45, London Road, next to Terrace Lane. Residents were Ronald Arch, Francis Frost, Frederick Bennison, John Hooks, Ernest Grimes and Sydney Jubey.

RIGHT & BELOW: Whitehouse Cottages, from 26, London Road. Residents were Mrs Ives, Miss Sayer, Harry Collison, Wilfred Williams and Charles Rudd.

Garden Row, between 18 & 22, Windsor Road. This ran beside the Live and Let Live pub whose landlord was George
Ollett.Householders here were George Colby, Alexander Seapey, Albert Rose, Eleanor Broughton & George Elmer.
At the bottom of the Row was the old London Road Brewery.

ABOVE: 1 to 4, Hospital Walk. Harry Holland, Eric Smith, Henry Watson & William Capps lived here.
BELOW: Keppel Street. This ran from 4, Hospital Walk to 15, Windsor Road. Twenty seven families lived in this street.

RIGHT:
The map shows the area bounded
by London Road (bottom right corner),
Checker Street, Southgate Street and Friar's
Street (off the map to the left).

BELOW:
Spencer's Square from 19, Checker Street.
Living here were Thomas Lambert,
Robert Nicholls, Wilfred Plumb,
Ernest Gray, Florence Nobbs,
William Greenacre, Thomas Edwards,
William Day and Mary Nicholls.
.

ABOVE: Spencer's Square. This shows Nos. 3, 4 & 5. No.3 on the left of the picture was the home of Ernest Gray, No.4 was the home of Florence Nobbs & No.5 the home of William Greenacre.
BELOW: Spencer's Square. This picture shows Nos.7 (William Day), 8 (Mary Nicholl) & 9 (Thomas Lambert).

ABOVE: Chessons Yard, from 2, Checker Street. Residents were Alice Jubey and William Allard.

ABOVE & BELOW: Evett's Yard, from 37, Checker Street.

ABOVE: Broughton's Cottages, at 43, Checker Street. Ernest Dunkley and Mrs Sutton lived here. RIGHT: Fleece Yard, Friars Street.

Fleece Yard, from 55, Friars Street. One shy young lady hides her face while everyone else poses for the cameraman.
Residents here at this time were Mrs Clark, John Steinford, Jas Bussey, Mrs Gamble, Alfred William Mitchell, Alfred Ernest Mitchell and Albert Clare.

ABOVE: Kemble's Yard, between 75 and 77, Friars Street. The house on the left is No.5 and named 'The Retreat'. Estella Griffin lived here. Other occupants in the yard were Ernest Barber & Bertie Smith.
BELOW: Kemble's Yard. An audience watches cycle repairs being carried out.

ABOVE: Begley's Yard, between 67 & 69, Friars Street. This yard was home to Robert Winter, Gertrude Carter, Herbert Francis & Henry Shorting.

LEFT & RIGHT: Plowright's Yard, from 13, Friars Street. Home of George Painter, Mrs S Oakes and Ernest Rye.

ABOVE: Horsley's Court, Southgate Street. Living here were Violet Bowen, Matthew Chapman, Elizabeth Ashton & Ruth Gibson.
BELOW: Southgate Court, Southgate Street.

ABOVE & BELOW: Southgate Court, from 2, Southgate Street. Residents were Sarah Pratt, Jessie Suitor, William Potter, James Dexter, Arthur West, Edith Shepheard, Frederick Britton, Harry Funnell, James Curson & Robert Funnell.

ABOVE:
Front Row, Highgate. Approximately forty families lived in Front Row.
The picture was taken from across the Gaywood River.

BELOW (Left & Right)
Further along was Stag Row, Highgate. Living here were Harry Frost, Arthur Cooper,
George Lake, Emma Fountain, Edith Collison, Kate Maxwell, Alice Benefer and Charles Manning.

Index

	Page			Page
All Saint's Street	62		Hildon's Yard	10
Anchor of Hope Yard	11		Horsley's Court	91
Arme's Yard	49,50		Hospital Walk	81
Atto's Yard	5		Johnson's Square	14
Baptist's Yard	45,46		Kemble's Yard	88
Bath's Yard	44		Kendrick's Yard	53
Begley's Yard, Friars Street	89		Keppel Street	81
Begley's Yard, North Street	18,19		Law's Yard, Bridge Street	67
Bennett's Yard, St. Nicholas Street	30		Law's Yard, High Street	51,52
Bennett's Yard, Tower Street	48		Lift's Yard	11
Bird's Yard	23		Lincoln's Yard	54
Bone's Yard	56		Little Chequer	55
Bridge Street	61		May Cottages	55
Broughton's Cottages	86		Miles Court	32
Browning's Yard	9		Miller's Court	68
Brown's Yard	57		Mill's Yard	38,39
Burrell's Yard	28		Mount Pleasant	40
Burton's Court	48		North End Yard	27
California Yard	6,7		North Everard Place	75,76
Chapel Buildings	33		North Place	21
Chapel Yard, Pilot Street	23		Payne's Court	58
Chapel Yard, St. Nicholas Street	30		Pilot Street	26
Chesson's Yard	84		Plowright's Yard	90
Churchman's Yard	21		Providence Street	71
Colby's Yard	72		Pump Yard	68
Crisp's Yard	63		Purfleet Street	54
Crome's Yard	67		Railway Passage	16
Crooked Lane	64		Ravenshaw's Yard	33
Cross Lane	36,37		Rhodes Yard	24
Cross Yard	34		Rutter's Yard	15
Daisley's Buildings	70		Sacker's Yard	28
Dennis Yard	53		Seed's Yard	29
Devonshire's Yard	20		Simpson's Yard	63
Dye's Building	74		Skipper's Yard	35
East Anglia Place	72,73		Softley's Yard	47
East Place	12		Southgate Court	91,92
Edward's Yard	31		Spencer's Square	82,83
Evett's Yard	85		St. John's Cottages	77
Fleece Yard	86,87		Stag Row	93
Front Row	93		Stanley Square	43
Frost's Yard	77		Stonegate Street	60
Garden Row	80		Surrey Square	46
Garland Yard	12		Tower Court	58
Gazley's Yard	8		Trundle's Yard	42
George Yard	13,14		Union Place	65,66
Gilbert's Row	78		Valentine's Yard	5
Grampus Yard	25		Vicarage Lane	69
Half Moon Yard	27		Watson's Yard	19
Hanover Yard	22		Whincop Place	41,42
Hanwell's Yard	22		Whitehouse Cottages	79
Harrod's Yard	71		Whitening Yard	17,18
Hart's Yard	25		Wilson's Flats, Broad Street	43

Appendix

The photographs on this and the following page have been included even though I have been unable to identify the locations. The quality of print is also inferior compared with the rest of the pictures in this book. Having said that, I felt it would be a shame to leave them out as I'm sure that they will be identified by others!